D0973000

Every disabled person has the choice
of either 'crying the blues' about their
disability every day of their life, or realistically
acknowledging what they have to do in
order to have a successful, productive life.

The Disability Rag

Job-Hunting Tips
For The So-Called Handicapped
or People Who Have Disabilities

A Supplement To
What Color Is Your Parachute?

by
Richard Nelson Bolles
Author, *What Color Is Your Parachute?*

Ten Speed Press

Ten Speed Press
P.O. Box 7123
Berkeley, California 94707

Cover painting is "The Knave" by Maxfield Parrish (American: 1870 - 1966). Oil on board. Private collection. Photograph courtesy of the Alma Gilbert Galleries in Burlingame, California. The photo is from the illustration in the *Knave of Hearts 1989 Engagement Book* published by Pomegranate Books by arrangement with Alma Gilbert.

ISBN 0-89815-471-5

Library of Congress Cataloging-in-Publication Data

Bolles, Richard Nelson.
 Job-hunting tips for the so-called handicapped or people who have disabilities : a supplement to What color is your parachute? / by Richard Nelson Bolles.
  p. cm.
 Includes bibliographical references.
 ISBN 0-89815-471-5 : $5.95
 1. Vocational guidance for the handicapped—United States.
2. Handicapped—Employment—United States. 3. Job hunting—United States. I. Bolles, Richard Nelson. What color is your parachute?
 Supplement. II. Title.
HV1568.5.B85 1991
650. 14'087—dc20   91-38506
              CIP

Printed in the United States of America

1 2 3 4 5 — 95 94 93 92 91

Foreword

A Short Course On Disabilities
For Those Of Us Who Do Not (Yet)
Have A Disability.

A disability is traditionally defined as *any impairment of some major life activity, that lasts six months or longer.* Typically, it is a permanent impairment. There are, by the most recently published government census (August, 1989), 13.4 million working-age people in this country who have such an impairment of a major life activity. When to these are added those *under* age 16 or *over* age 64 who have disabilities, the total population of persons with disabilities is commonly estimated to be between 43 and 50 million--though no one knows how to get an exact count.

Vocabulary is very important to people with disabilities. Generalizations are difficult to make, because vocabulary is hotly debated even within the disabled community. But, *as a general rule,* they prefer to be called "people..." or "a person with a disability," thus making them **a person primarily,** and one with a disability secondarily. "Disabled" is second on their list of preferred terms. "Handicapped" has come into great disfavor, although of course it remains up, in many public signs. (Also, managers in various companies often use the term "handicapped" to characterize those already disabled before they begin working at that company, while they reserve the term "disabled" for those who were not disabled when they were hired but became disabled *on the job.*)

Those *in* a wheelchair now generally prefer to be called "those who *use* a chair," since 75% of those who use a chair can get up and move out of it. The former "mentally retarded" now prefer to be called "cognitively disabled." The former "mentally ill" now prefer to be called "emotionally disabled" or "psychiatrically disabled" or "the stabilized mentally ill." The former "physically handicapped" now generally prefer to be called "functionally disabled." The blind generally prefer to be called "people who are blind," though some who are not totally blind prefer "visually impaired," "partially sighted," or "print impaired." The deaf generally prefer to be called "people who are deaf," though some who are not totally deaf prefer "a person with a hearing impairment."

About 36% of men with disabilities who are of working age (16-64) are in the labor force *or actively seeking work*; for disabled women that figure is 28%. This means 64% of disabled men and 72% of disabled women are *not* in the labor force. These latter percentages are often quoted as the unemployment rate among people with disabilities, though technically one is unemployed only if one *wants* to work, but cannot *find* employment. Nonetheless, even with some allowance for this fact, people with disabilities remain **the group with by far the highest unemployment rate in the U.S. today.** One in five adults with a work disability falls below the poverty line. Experts say that with the necessary support, *at least* 5 million more people with disabilities between the ages of 16 and 64 could be working and want to work. This, of course, represents an untapped labor pool which employers will *have* to pay attention to, along with minorities and the elderly, *if* the labor shortage that has long been predicted, does in fact materialize during the 1990s.

Before this untapped **labor pool** of people with disabilities can be utilized, employers will have to discard many of the myths they believe without thinking -- such as: "People who are retarded can only do single-step repetitious tasks, and they don't mind." Or: "The kind of work people who are deaf should do is work in noisy rooms." Or: "The only place people who are blind can really flourish is in darkrooms."

It is instructive to consider the kinds of jobs people with disabilities actually hold. Let us take people who are blind as an example. The kind of full-time jobs they hold down, include: artists, auto mechanics, ballerinas, beekeepers, bicycle repair people, boat builders, carpenters, chiropractors, college professors, counselors (drug/alcohol/youth/marriage), court reporters, dispatchers for 911 or for transportation companies, fingerpainters, fish-cleaners, food service management, inventors, lawyers, licensed practical nurses, machinists, managers of snack stands and cafeterias in federal and other government buildings, marketing specialists, massage therapists, medical and legal transcribers, models (on runways as well as for magazines), musicians, packagers/assemblers in all kinds of manufacturing, painters, peanut vendors in stands at basketball or football games, professional story tellers, psychiatrists, public relations people, sculptors, strippers, teachers, word processing and data entry people, writers -- and various kinds of self-employment. And this is only a sampling.

What kinds of salaries do people with disabilities make? Well, male workers with disabilities who are working full-time averaged $24,200 in annual salary during 1987, while female workers in the same category averaged $15,796. *These figures equalled 81% and 84% respectively, of what their nondisabled counterparts earned, on average, in 1987. (These ratios were a drop from the 91% and 88% ratios attained as recently as 1980.) This disparity (between wages offered a person without a disability and a person with a disability) is shown most dramatically by how a person with a new disability is treated, once they become disabled. For example, a roofer earning $40,000 from his employer before a disabling accident, may be offered as little as $12,000* **after** *the accident.*

While the *average salary earned* seems respectable, it must be set over against the economic **disincentives** for *ever* going to work, once one has a disability and is receiving some sort of disability payments from one's former employer, the State or the Federal government. These disincentives include: **the loss of sizeable medical insurance** which one may have been receiving from disability insurance or State/Federal programs (e.g., SSDI -- Social Security Disability Insurance, or SSI -- Supplemental Security Income) -- though by Federal Law #1619A and #1619B, Medicaid cannot be eliminated, *if* an individual has no other insurance; **the cost of transportation to work,** especially for severely disabled individuals -- *which incidentally is not tax-deductible, though it is deductible as Impairment Related Work Expense when Social Security is figuring out by how much to reduce SSDI/SSI payments;* **the inability to get similar insurance from one's new employer,** since private insurance companies will *never* cover 'pre-existing conditions'; **the fact that even if one finds a job, one faces a mandatory**

time gap of two years between the time one may lose the job *(due to 'downsizing,' 'hostile takeovers,' or being fired)* and the time that one's old State/Federal medical insurance can be reinstated; and to these economic disincentives we may add: **the lack of physical access in many workplaces that are** *otherwise* **attractive places for employment; and lack of public transportation for the severely disabled** (especially for those who use wheelchairs and have no van or car).

What all this adds up to is that a person with a disability may receive less total income (including medical payments) if they go to work, than if they stayed home. Nonetheless, people with disabilities *still* elect to seek work, even when it is economically disadvantageous to them to do so -- even as people from 'the private sector' may go into government service, despite a similar loss of income. When people with disabilities do so, at such personal cost, it is usually because of the driving need they feel to put their God-given abilities into the service of mankind. And, secondarily, because of their need to maintain or increase their own sense of self-worth, as well as prevent their skills from deteriorating simply through disuse.

It is certainly to our nation's advantage to have every person with a disability in the work force, for the costs to the nation of their *not* working are these: the loss of the taxes they would otherwise pay; the loss of the money they would otherwise put into the economy, through their **purchases** of life's necessities; the loss of the **family income and taxes,** where family members are forced to take part-time work or give up work altogether; and the cost of **government funds** to support the unemployed person who has a disability.

While throughout this booklet, I have spoken of "people with disabilities" as though they were one "tribe," there is in actual fact no such thing as a *typical* disabled person. As experts point out, every disability is a mix of three things: **An Event** (the disability), **The Individual** (his or her attitude, resources, etc.), and **The Environment** (how friendly or barring it is to that disability, how much support it offers that Individual). The outcome of that mix will vary widely from one disabled person to another. The chart on the facing page, however, shows *something* of the immense varieties of disability.

Not mentioned in this chart are the varying *causes* of any particular disability. For example, if we see someone using a wheelchair, their "impairment of motion" may be due to: amputation after an auto accident, arthritis, cerebral palsy, epilepsy, muscular dystrophy, polio, spina bifida, spinal cord injuries, etc.

What do these varying causes signify? They signify that disability is not like race, or stature, or your birthplace. Where you were born, will always be so. Your race and your stature also will not change. But whether or not you are one of "the so-called handicapped or disabled," can change during the next twenty-four hours. Five out of every six people with disabilities were NOT born with that disability, but acquired it later in life. *New* causes of disability are constantly appearing; among those in the news during the past five years or so: AIDS (of course), Lyme disease, repetitive strain injury, carpal tunnel syndrome and chronic fatigue syndrome (CFS).

All of us, therefore, are only one incident away from joining this group of "people with disabilities." You can become

No Two Disabled Persons Are Alike

Each One is a PERSON who has a disability
that has one of the characteristics on each line below:*

HIDDEN i.e., not immediately apparent to others		**VISIBLE** i.e., immediately or quickly apparent to others	

MILD	MODERATE	SEVERE	PROFOUND

CONGENITAL i.e., it occurred either at birth or before they were 5	**ADVENTITIOUS** i.e., it came *(advent)* into their life after they were 5

Their impairment only limits their ability to:

SEE	HEAR	SPEAK	MOVE	THINK OR LEARN	FEEL OR BEHAVE	OTHER	More than one of the previous

With respect to their abilities in other areas:

THEY ARE NORMALLY GIFTED in other areas	THEY ARE EXTRAORDINARILY GIFTED in one or more other areas

Their attitude toward their disability is:

THEY SEE IT AS A DISASTER which has overwhelmed them	THEY SEE IT AS A CHALLENGE for them to overcome

Their driving motive in life *(besides survival)* is their desire for:

AFFILIATION or the need to relate to people	ACHIEVEMENT or the need to outdo their own record	EXCELLING or the need to outdo others

In dealing with their disability they are:

SOCIALLY ISOLATED hence, dealing with it essentially on their own	SOCIALLY SUPPORTED hence, dealing with it with help from others

In dealing with their **abilities** they are:

UNAWARE of what they can do, and do well, and enjoy	WELL AWARE of what they can do, and do well, and enjoy

N.B. The categories on one line are NOT necessarily related to the categories immediately below it.

permanently disabled with one accident at home, one falling --
on an icy step, on a slippery sidewalk, on a newly waxed floor,
down a flight of stairs, off a ladder, off a roof, on a ski slope,
on an amateur playing field -- one unexpected crippling illness
(arthritis, heart disease, among others), one auto accident, one
encounter with the wrong insect, or virus, or chemical agent.
And this booklet which you read today out of curiosity or
compassion for others, may tomorrow become words you
need for your very own life.

R.N.B.

Rules About Job-Hunting

Unless you are going to create your own job, looking for work is essentially a matter of finding out about a job, and then **competing** for it. That's true for *anybody*. If you are a person who happens to have a disability, what is different is that you face *tougher* competition. The rules that apply to all job-hunters therefore apply to you in double measure. You *must* arm yourself as best you can for the competition you will face. There are hurdles or obstacles you must overcome, both 'out there' and inside yourself.

Your main obstacles 'out there' are (of course) the ignorance, fear, anxiety, prejudice, and discrimination that you will run into with employers or your future co-workers. Much of this is based on ignorance which *you* will have to dispel yourself. **As a disabled job-hunter, part of your task in job-hunting is that you will** *often* **have to educate would-be employers, as you go.**

The main obstacle 'inside yourself' will be the temptation to feel hopelessness. This is based, obviously, on what you already know about the nature of the world of work. Or, rather, on *what you think you know*. The sad truth is, that many of us with disabilities do ourselves believe the damaging myths that 'the world' out there believes, and uses to justify not hiring us.

And what are those myths? Their nature is evident if you just examine *the dark thoughts* that those of us with disabilities often have, when first we set out job-hunting. We compare ourselves, of course, with those who *don't* have any observable disabilities, and it comes out sounding like this:

I am disabled, they are not; *I am probably unemployable,* they are not; *I am filled with a sense of what I cannot do,* while they are filled with a sense of what they can do; *I am set apart from the rest of mankind,* they are not; *I have nothing in common with an employer,* while they do; *I have to ask the employer to redesign the job to accommodate my limitations,* while they do not.

All of these thoughts are common, all of these thoughts are understandable, but *all of these thoughts are untrue.* Moreover, treating them as though they *were* true, will inevitably cause the hopelessness you are trying to avoid.

If you examine **the true nature of the job-hunt,** you will discover that there are four reasons for you to be hopeful. Don't assume that these are commonly understood 'out there.' Mind you, these are *the very four things* that you will probably have to educate employers and others about, as you go. So, get them *very* clear in *your* mind before you go out job-hunting:

Four Reasons for Hope

That Are Important To Those Of Us With Disabilities (As Well As To Our Would-Be Employers, Counselors, Friends, and Family)

> **1.** **Everyone is disabled. And, everyone is employable.**

Let us suppose the human race had a Skills Bank, in which there was a total of 13,000 skills, and each one of us at birth had to go to that bank and choose 700 skills that we would use for the rest of our life here on earth. You and I, of course, would not choose the same 700. *You* might choose to be good at *analyzing things*, while *I* might choose to be good at *drawing*. And so forth. The varying skills we chose would make us different from one another, even unique.

But, how would you describe yourself, afterward? Would you point to the 700 things you can do, and do well? If so, you would be emphasizing **your abilities.** Or would you point to the 12,300 things that you still can't do - - even if some *other* members of the human race can? If so, you would be emphasizing **your disabilities.**

The point of this little exercise is: *everyone* has abilities, or things we *can* do. And *everyone* has disabilities, or things we *can't* do. *(The numbers 700 and 13,000 were only chosen for the sake of illustration. No one actually knows how many skills the human race has, or how many a typical individual has.)*

The numbers are unimportant. The *principle* is what is important:

Everyone is **enabled,** and everyone is also **disabled.**

Everyone is **free,** and everyone is also **handicapped.** That's the nature of the life that is given to us.

If you speak of yourself only as free, enabled, and as a person with abilities, you are denying *the other side* of your nature. Or if you speak of yourself only as handicapped, disabled, and as a person with disabilities, you are denying the first side of your nature. Each and every human being is both sides.

In interpreting yourself to an employer, it is crucial for you to know this and emphasize this during an interview. You can put it quite simply, *"It's true I have a disability; all of us do. Everyone of us has things he or she cannot do well. But I am here because there are many things I can do, and do well. This is what they are...."* It is these abilities of yours that make you *eminently employable.* Of course, to be able to say what they are, you *must* have done your homework on yourself, and know *what* it is you can do and do well.

If you want the employer to think of you as both enabled and disabled--just like every other human being--*you must think of yourself that way too.* And be able to spell it out, in detail. Therein lies your hope.

2. Everyone is a member of many "tribes," and as a general rule employers like to hire those whom they perceive to be members of their own "tribe."

Since disability is a characteristic of us all, it follows from this that your disability ought never to stand in the way of your finding employment. Unfortunately--as we all know too well--it sometimes does, and those of us who happen to have obvious disabilities need to know why.

The "why" seems obvious. We run into an obstacle, which is normally called "prejudice" or "discrimination." Trouble is, while this description is true, as far as it goes, it doesn't go anywhere near far enough. Thus it ends up being a woefully inadequate description of our enemy. And when you don't know your enemy, it is almost impossible to win.

The truest description of the enemy we face in the job-hunt (and elsewhere) is **tribalism.** So, understanding tribalism is crucial to the success of your job-hunt. I am not here speaking of "tribes" as understood by Native Americans; I am speaking in a more universal sense.

A "tribe" is any group that gives individuals a feeling of **"we,"** as opposed to all *the others* out there, who are **"them."** From way back in our history, we who are human have always tended to organize ourselves into "tribes," both in our thinking and in actuality.

"Them," "the others," may be variously defined as those who belong to a different race, a different religious group, a different nationality, a different social status, or a different economic status, than we do.

Each of us usually belongs to *several* "tribes." Our commitment to one "tribe" may be merely that of sympathy for others who are "like us"--in this way or that; while our commitment to another "tribe" may be one of fierce loyalty and action unto the death, as in a clan or in a terrorist group.

"Tribes" come in all sizes and shapes. They may be as local as a neighborhood, or as worldwide as a religion. They may be as small as a group of "buddies," or as large as a nation, flaunting fierce patriotism. We see them in clubs, we see them at sporting events, we see them at rallies, we see them at conventions, we see them in political parties, we see them in issues like abortion, we see them when families gather at holidays, and we see them in drug gangs.

While "tribes" *can* perform truly nobly--they will sometimes give their own members sacrificial devotion and kindness--on the whole, tribalism has created the darkest pages of mankind's history. Ethics which normally govern daily conduct are tossed out the window when dealing with other "tribes." *One "tribe" is often singled out for particular contempt,* disdain, epithets, hatred and even physical violence. Consider what we see in Ireland, Beirut, Eastern Europe, Palestine, the former Soviet Union, and of course our own country, with its racism, ageism, prejudice and discrimination.

Even when "tribes" are rather benign in their conduct, they are rarely accused of showing any *sensitivity* to the needs or feelings of those who are not members of that "tribe."

Tribalism not only devastates human relations, it alters the landscape. In any particular geographic area, we see

the dominant "tribe" shaping the landscape and the environment to its own liking and its own needs, without much consideration for the other "tribes" who may be living off the same land. We call this insensitive dominance one of "handicapping" the other "tribe" or "tribes." Forcing the other "tribes" to live in a harsh landscape *so far as the needs of those "tribes" are concerned,* the dominant "tribe" usually then thinks of, or calls, the other "tribes" *the handicapped.*

In our country, of course, the dominant "tribe" in charge of human relations, the landscape, and the environment, are the people who have no real impairment of 'any major life activity'--in other words, *people without disabilities.* This "tribe" treats *the others* with great insensitivity, disdain, fear, and sometimes contempt and animosity. Naturally, this "tribe" has designed its roads, its transportation, its buildings, its doorways, its stairways, its workplaces, its amusement centers, and its bathrooms to suit itself. Needless to say, those who do not belong to this "tribe," those who do have some impairment of 'a major life activity,' *the others,* *"them,"* often find it difficult to get around or to work, in that inimical environment.

"Tribes," in addition to undermining human relations, and altering the landscape, usually create their own distinctive language. And so it is that the dominant "tribe" in this country, referred to above, has a language which describes themselves as: *we,* "people with abilities," "normal," or "the able-bodied"; while they call all the other "tribes" who *have* some impairment to 'a major life activity': *the others, them,* "people with disabilities," "the disabled" or "the handicapped." It would of course be more accurate if they called us: "those whom we have handicapped by the way we have shaped our environment."

Here endeth our brief course on tribalism. Now, what does all this have to do with our job-hunt? Simply this: when those of us who happen to have disabilities go out job-hunting, we are unconsciously perceived as one "tribe" trying to find employment from another "tribe." And the more *visible* our disability is--that is, the *more* we are perceived as looking *different* from the dominant "tribe" (people without disabilities)--the more *some* employers will feel the force of this. And since as a general rule **employers like to hire those whom they perceive to be members of their own "tribe,"** this is not good news. But it can be turned into good news, if you put your thinking cap on. Used rightly, tribalism can become the key to your getting hired.

As I said earlier, everyone is a member of **many** "tribes." Therefore, the key to your having a successful job interview is to ignore "tribes" defined by ability or disability, and **find instead some other "tribe"** in which both you and your would-be employer are members.

Did you both grow up in the same town?--then you are members of *that* same "tribe." Did you both go to the same school?--then you are members of *that* same "tribe." Do you both have the same hobbies?--then you are members of *that* same "tribe." Have you both traveled to the same places?--then you are members of *that* same "tribe." Or do you both share the same interest?--then you are members of *that* same "tribe."

It is remarkable how many people know instinctively how important it is to establish this kinship in the same "tribe." Recently the roof of our vacation cottage in Oregon needed repairing, and when the doorbell rang, this is how the roofer began the conversation with my wife: "Carol? How are you? I'm Bill, from the roofing people. Hey, I hear you folks are from Walnut Creek. Is that true? Well, you know, I was born in the very next town, and I grew up there all my boyhood. You know where Monument Boulevard is in Pleasant Hill? Well, that's where I grew up...." In approaching an employer, your job is to make this same kind of connection.

This will be easier if you do enough research on that employer *before you go in* so you have discovered some commonality between you. If you can't discover any such, *before* the interview, then *that discovery* must be your goal *during* the interview. Once that employer feels that you are both members of *some* "tribe," in common - - despite your disability - - you will have secured that most important of all qualities in a job-interview: **rapport between you and the employer.** And this rapport is **the key** to your getting hired. Because, as I said, employers like to hire those whom they perceive to be somehow members of their own "tribe."

---

3. Employers never hire a stranger.

Almost every job-hunter who happens to have a disability wants to find some magical way of avoiding going face-to-face with employers. (So do most job-hunters who *don't* have a disability, incidentally.) Of course we know that job-hunters *have* to go face-to-face. But we hope that maybe we can plead our disability as a reason to be let off the hook, on this one. Especially if our disability is one of limited mobility. Perhaps *we* will be allowed to just communicate with the would-be employer by letter or by telephone?

No such luck! You may do some *preliminary* explorations by letter or telephone, if you wish; but in the end you will *have* to go face-to-face. And risk rejection. Just like every other job-hunter. You too, in a series of job-interviews, may hear the unnerving refrain - - you will find the refrain in *What Color Is Your Parachute?* - - NO NO NO

NO NO NO NO NO NO NO NO YES YES. It applies to those of us who happen to have disabilities, just as much as it does to those of us who don't happen to have disabilities (yet).

The reason why you *have* to go face-to-face with a would-be employer, in spite of the possibility of rejection, is that *employers never hire a stranger.* Nathan Azrin was the first to emphasize this *(see the bibliography at the end of this booklet).* What it means is, that in order to decide to hire you, employers have to:

a) see you,

b) like you,

c) be convinced that there is something you can
    do for them,

d) and then feel that because of that, they've *got*
    to have you.

Notice the importance of c) and d). *Some* of us with disabilities think it only takes a) and b). *"Did you get the job?"* "Yes, I did." *"Why did you get hired?"* "Because she liked me." Or: *"Did you get turned down for the job?"* "Yes, I did." *"Why did you get turned down?"* "Because he didn't like me."

Actually, the employer may have liked you a great deal. But if you couldn't tell him (or her) what you could do for them, then *that* is why you got turned down. Few if any employers are ever going to take the time to do this homework for you. That is not their responsibility.

It's important to recall just what a job *is.* In the beginning, some man or woman decides to go into business for themselves. They want to sell a product, or information, or a service to others. To make this business succeed, they initially do *everything* themselves: making the product, or offering the service, or gathering the information all by their lonesome. In time, the business prospers, and it gets to be too much for one person to do. Our hero or heroine needs help.

What kind of help? Well, first of all they need someone to come and offer them **their time.** But they don't just need time. They need someone who, in that time, can **do the things they need to have done.** Maybe they have no time or skills, themselves, to keep their accounting books. So they need someone to come and help them who knows how to do accounting, and has the time. In exchange for that time and those accounting skills, our hero or heroine is willing to give something in return: **money.** In other words, some of their profits. This exchange turns them into an employer, and the other person into their employee. And so, a job is born.

But: employers never hire a stranger. You must go face-to-face. And, you must help them to know you, *at least a little,* in the interview--before they will be willing to offer you a job. How can you help them to know you? By telling them who you are: that is, what your abilities or skills are, and thus, what you have to offer them that would persuade them to part with some of their money.

Oops, you haven't thought about that? You were only focussed on your **disability,** trying to think of how to get them to ignore it? *Tilt.* No job. You were too focussed on *who you are not,* rather than on who you are; too focussed on what you can't do, rather than on what you can do.

A bit of advice: go home, and before you visit any other employer, be sure you sit down and figure out what you do well. If you can't figure this out by yourself, for one reason or another, get a mate, a friend, a counselor, to help you. Then, next time you go for an interview, you will be ready to tell your would-be employer *who you are,* in terms of your abilities, or skills. *Good.* Because, as I said, employers never hire a stranger.

---

4. Everyone redesigns or modifies their job so as to highlight their abilities and get around their limitations.

It is common for those of us who have disabilities to think that when we go job-hunting, we are going to have to request something unheard of in the world of work: namely, that the job be redesigned, to accommodate our special limitations. *Wrong.*

As Sidney Fine has emphasized, *everyone* redesigns or modifies their job--in minor ways or major. The reason for this is that no job exactly fits anyone, when they are first hired. Their new job is like an ill-fitting suit. Inevitably, it *has* to be taken in, a tuck here, a tuck there; or it has to be let out, where it is pinching or hugging too tight --before the person is able to do their best in that job. All of us have to alter, adjust, amend, revise, fine tune, adapt, or shape each new job, in minor ways or major.

For example, let us say that a nondisabled person gets a job on an assembly line, where he is supposed to continually pick up a carton from a whole stack of them that stands to his right. But he is left-handed. So, he redesigns his work space, and moves the stack of cartons over to the left side, in order that he may pick them up more handily. *He has redesigned or modified his job so as to highlight his abilities, and get around his limitations--but no one thinks anything of it.*

Or, again, let us say a nondisabled person is an executive. Her predecessor always called her subordinates into her office, and listened to their verbal summary of what they needed her decisions on. But *this* executive is more of *an eye person* than *an ear person*. She doesn't absorb their verbal summaries very well, when she is only able to hear them. So she redesigns their encounters, and asks them in addition to their verbal reports to her, to give her a one-page written summary of what they want her decisions on, and wait until she has had a chance to read them. *She has redesigned or modified her job so as to highlight her abilities, and get around her limitations--but no one thinks anything of it.*

Not just employees but employers also have gotten into this business of redesigning jobs--to get around the limitations of their employees. And often new technology has to be brought into play. For example, when employers realized that many of the employees they would have to hire couldn't add or subtract, they redesigned cash registers so that these told the employee what change to give back to the customer, once they had keyed in the amount handed over, by the customer. When employers in fast-food places realized that many of the employees they would have to hire couldn't read, they redesigned cash registers with pictures of the food, instead of words. When employers realized many of the employees they would have to hire couldn't remember instructions, they designed cash registers with screens over them that displayed the proper instructions, such as "Close drawer." (I saw this at Macy's recently.) Yet again, when employers discovered that people on assembly lines couldn't read blueprints, they fashioned 'exploded drawings.'

And so we see that redesigning jobs, in order to accommodate the limitations of the person holding down that job, goes on *all the time* in the world of work. It goes on without anyone even batting an eye, or thinking about it--until, of course, we *who happen to have some obvious disability* walk in, asking for a job there. Then, when it becomes obvious that the price of hiring us is that the job will have to be partially redesigned or modified so as to highlight our abilities and get around our limitations-- perhaps with some new technology, as above--the employer often acts as though we were asking for something no other job-hunter asks for.

You have to tell him (or her). Tell them gently. Tell them nicely. But *tell* them: "*Employers and employees* continually redesign or modify jobs, so as to highlight employees' abilities and get around their limitations." Same goes for you; *no big deal.*

You will be way ahead of the competition if, in addition to this general assurance, you can indicate more particularly **which tasks** you and the employer will need to redesign. *This will be relatively easy if* before you approach the employer for an interview, you first conduct conversations elsewhere with workers who actually do the work you would like to do.

One way of approaching such fellow workers is to say, "I need to come in and talk to somebody with your expertise, who can tell me if a person with my abilities, and my disability, can work in this particular field or industry." Your goal during such conversations is to find out the various tasks that make up that job, *and* what skills it takes to do those tasks. Then you can isolate the **problem tasks** (for you). These will be the areas where you need to figure out some job redesigning. Your friends (or counselor) should be able to brainstorm this with you *before* you ever go in to see prospective employers for the particular kind of job that you are interested in.

If you *aren't* able to do this ahead of time, you might say to the employer, "Could you please give me an idea of how you have designed this job in your organization, and what tasks it requires to be done." Then you may break down the job into which tasks you are perfectly able to do, and which tasks you and they would need to redesign.

Well, there are the four principles that are the ground of hope for you, in your job-hunt. If you feel more hopeful, now that these are clear in your mind, that empowers you. And you do want to feel empowered, strengthened, encouraged, or self-actualized, when you go about the job-hunt. For, the basic principle of all job-hunting is: **if you want something to happen, it is you who must make it happen--with God's help.** That's as true for those of us with disabilities as it is for the nondisabled job-hunter.

This brings us then to our next question:

What Do You Need to Do, After Finding Hope?

Hopefully, now, you have identified a job (or jobs) you can do--where **your particular disability is no barrier** to doing *that* job well. If you're having trouble identifying such a job, ask yourself, "What is it that I most want to do with my life?" If you're still having trouble, ask yourself, "What is it that no one else in my area wants to do, sell, offer, or make, that I would love to do, sell, offer, or make?"

Once you've identified such a job that you might like to do, go talk to someone with a disability who is doing it. In fact, talk to several people with disabilities who are doing it. Pick their brains for everything you can.

Some agencies maintain lists of such people. For example, the American Foundation for the Blind maintains *The Job Index*, a list of actual jobs held by persons who are blind; if you also are blind or have a sight impairment, the Index people can link you to someone who is doing the job you think you might like to do. *(Their address is Job Index, American Foundation for the Blind, 15 West 16th St., New York, NY 10011, 212-620-2055.)*

You may decide, after talking to such workers, that you want to do this thing on your own. But if you want to work for someone else, this is where you set out to identify employers who have such jobs. In this information search, pay particular attention to employers with twenty or less employees, as that is where two-thirds of all new jobs are created.

During this information gathering, you may stumble across employers who give special advantage to people with disabilities. San Jose, California, for example, has (at this writing) a temporary agency, PROJECT HIRE, that sends people with disabilities out to jobs. Again, many states give an exemption to people with severe disabilities who want to work for the federal or state government, so that they do not have to go through civil service lists.

When you find employers that interest you, you will need to approach them. (As we said previously, employers never hire strangers.) During the interview, you need to be quietly assertive and persistent about what you want.

The main thing to remember during your interview

with *any* employer, is that **every employer has fears,** and much of your task during the job-interview is to try to put these fears to rest. You, of course, want to know what *particular* fears the employer is likely to entertain because you have a disability. So, let's open that Pandora's box.

The Fears An Employer Has
When Interviewing People With Disabilities

If only you could read the employers' thoughts, this is what you might hear:

"I don't exactly understand what this person's disability is, and I'm afraid to ask." *You have to figure out how to disarm this fear.* You will not help matters if you merely stand and deliver the title of your disability. The employer may still be as mystified as before, and *still* afraid to ask. Instead, before you ever go into an interview, you should practice writing down or dictating into an audiocassette the answers to these four questions, until you know them by heart:

1. "What is it that I can do, and do well?"
2. "What is it that I can't do?"
3. "What can I tell them about the ways or strategies I have developed for getting around my limitations?" *For example, if you are a person who is deaf, telling them that you always carry a notepad and pencil around with you.*
4. "What is it that I have learned *through* my disability?" e.g., *if you've trained attendants, you have experience in training people.*

Then when you are face-to-face with an employer, simply find an opportune time in the interview to recite these four things, in exactly that order, and this should put *that* fear to rest, forever. Next fear?

"Will my insurance go up, if I hire this person?" *You have to figure out how to disarm this fear.* This is probably the most common fear among employers, and also the one that is *least* based on facts. Knowledgeable people who work with disabilities do not know of one single insurance company or workperson's compensation program in this country that will raise its premiums if an insured employer hires someone with a disability. Next?

"What if I would like to hire this disabled person, but there is some problem about adapting this particular job to their limitations, and neither they nor I know how to solve that problem?" *You have to figure out how to disarm this fear.* To an employer who says, "I'd hire you, BUT....." you can say, "Could you please give me some idea of how you have designed this job in your organization? I feel quite confident that I could do the job in general. As for the particular tasks that might give me a problem, I'm usually able to figure out a way to get them accomplished. Just give me a few days to work on it."

There are helps for you in this, such as the Job Accommodation Network (JAN) funded by the President's Committee on Employment of People with Disabilities, and headquartered at the University of West Virginia, 809 Allen Hall, Morgantown, WV 26506. Their phone number is 800-526-7234. They also serve Canada, and the Canadian number is 1-800-526-2262. JAN is essentially a computerized database of job accommodation information (at *their* disposal, not yours). Anyone can call them: job-hunters, employers, or counselors. A job-hunter with a disability, such as yourself, might tell them, "I want to be hired as a _____, and I found a prospective employer, but they said the reason they won't hire me for that position is _____. Is there any gadget or tool or other strategy that would give me a solution to this problem?" JAN will ask you to describe:

The nature of your disability,

What the job is, and what tasks it requires you to perform,

What equipment they give you to perform the job with, and

What **problem** task remains, that you are asking JAN to help you figure some way around (some *functional accommodation,* to use the proper jargon).

JAN will search their database, and formulate strategies for dealing with the problem. Within 24 hours (usually) they will call you back or send you a summary which suggests devices, procedures or other ways of dealing with the problem you described to them. They will also send you information about the manufacturers of any devices they may suggest, and in some cases they may refer you to employers who have successfully dealt with this problem. There is no fee for this service.

Similar, though somewhat more specialized, assistance is provided by the IBM National Support Center for Persons with Disabilities, 800-IBM-2133, and the AT&T Special Needs Center, 800-233-1222, and the National Center on Employment of the Deaf, 716-475-6219.

If special equipment *is* needed in order for you to do that job, the Department or Bureau of Rehabilitation *(Voc*

Rehab) has enough funds in some States to purchase such equipment; in other States, it does not. Some States also have Worker Assistance Programs, funded by Private Industry Councils. Furthermore, if the employer decides to purchase the equipment, he or she is usually able to deduct such disability-related expenses from their taxes. The employer may also take money off his or her Federal taxes, just for hiring you, under the Federal Targeted Jobs Tax Credits provision. You may have to tell your would-be employer all of this. Also, you may have to get the necessary forms, for both yourself and the employer, when the time comes.

You may also need to tell them that in a recent survey (done by Lou Harris in 1987 for ICD--the International Center for the Disabled, in New York City), in companies which had hired disabled employees, three-fourths of all managers said that the average cost of employing a person with disabilities was about the same as the cost of employing someone without disabilities.

You can further tell them that eight out of ten line managers said disabled employees were no harder to support or supervise than were employees with no obvious disabilities. (For further information on the Lou Harris survey, see the ICD book mentioned in the bibliography at the end of this booklet.) Next?

"Just exactly how would this person get to work, here?" You have to figure out how to disarm this fear. It will help a lot if you've thought out some imaginative strategies ahead of time. For example, if you find a place that's willing to hire you but there is no public transportation to that

part of the city, and you don't have a car, consider alterna-
tives such as carpools, getting a ride with other employees
at that firm, asking if there is a company bus, etc.

**"What if I hire this disabled person, and they don't
work out? What if they quit? What if I have to fire them?
I'll be accused of firing them because they are disabled,
with maybe a lawsuit in the offing. I can't take that kind of
heat."** *You have to figure out how to disarm this fear.* People
with disabilities are not any more likely to need firing
than anyone else. In the Lou Harris survey alluded to previously, department heads and line managers *(in companies which had hired employees with disabilities)* gave their
disabled employees a *good* performance rating 64% of
the time, and an *excellent* performance rating 27% of the
time, with only 3% rating their job performance as fair,
and none evaluating it as poor. The survey concluded
"nearly all disabled employees do their jobs as well as or
better than other employees in similar jobs. They work as

hard or harder than nondisabled employees, and are as reliable and punctual or more so." So, what can you do? Well, generally speaking, you should anticipate the fear even before the employer mentions it, with some such words as these: "My injury (or disability) has been a blessing in disguise, because it's forced me to think out a career that I can do well and stay in permanently. If you're willing to take a chance on me, I'll give it my very best shot. But, if things don't work out to our mutual satisfaction, I'd want you to tell me *that* straight out; and I'll pick up my tent peaceably, and move on." Next fear?

"How is this disabled person going to get along with the other workers? What if my other employees are jealous of this new employee just because he or she does a superb job, and they feel that casts some aspersion on *them*? **What if I just** *have* **to promote him or her over the heads of other workers, on merit alone? I'm afraid that those who were passed over might attribute the promotion solely to my feeling sorry about this person's disability, rather than to their ability; and, if they're angry about it, may bring dissension into my workplace."** This is a well-grounded fear, since the Lou Harris survey revealed that at least 39% of all line managers *(in companies with disabled employees)* rated them as better than employees with no disabilities, in the areas of willingness to work hard, reliability, attendance and punctuality. *Still, you have to figure out how to disarm this fear.* Again, you may want to defuse this fear before it is even brought up, by saying something *like,* "Wherever I work, I tend to develop a natural rapport with my fellow-workers, so that they're rootin' for me as much as I'm rootin' for them."

"How is this disabled person going to communicate with others at work? I'm afraid that's going to be a serious difficulty." *You have to figure out how to disarm this fear.* It will help if you practice your answers ahead of time. For example, if you are a person who is deaf, you might say, "In the past, it hasn't been a problem. With friends and fellow-workers, I sometimes lip read, I sometimes write, and I also teach some simple sign language to them. It's worked out just fine."

"How will this disabled person avoid accidents on the job? I'm afraid he or she will be a safety hazard." *You have to figure out how to disarm this fear.* It is a significant one. Of those managers who had *not* hired any persons with disabilities during the past three years, 19% cited as the reason "disabled people being a safety risk to themselves and others." So, you *have* to figure out how to disarm this fear. Volunteering your own safety record, in the past, is of course one way to put this fear to rest. Also, you can point out that not only are you not a safety hazard, but you can actually contribute to better safety among the other employees. For example, if you are a person with a back injury who has had to learn proper lifting techniques, you can point out to the employer that you would be able to offer in-service training to the other employees about safe lifting techniques. And now, to the last fear.

"How will this disabled person handle emergencies, such as a fire in the building? I'm afraid they could get burned or killed, and I don't want that responsibility on my shoulders." *You have to figure out how to disarm this fear.* If you use a wheelchair, you can ask the employer to identify three nearby workers who could form a 'buddy' system with you, and help get you down the stairs in such an emergency.

And there you have it: the major fears employers have about hiring someone with a disability. Whatever words you come up with, to lay these fears at rest, be sure to use language that feels *natural* to you. Brainstorming with your family, or friends, or counselor, about this should help immeasurably.

When They Seem to Like You, But Won't Hire You

If you are interviewing at a place that interests you greatly, but it doesn't look like they are going to hire you, there is a plan B: *volunteer* your services, without pay, for a set time period at that place (two weeks to two months). *If* they take you up on this offer (they may not), this gives the employer a chance to look at your work *without any risk or cost*. There's *no* guarantee this will eventually get you a job there; but it is a strategy that *has* paid off many times for job-hunters. So it's certainly worth a shot, *if you can afford to do it*.

Volunteering may also be a winning strategy for you if you need to gain **experience** in the job-market, when you don't have any. *(In the Lou Harris survey, line managers said that a lack of past experience is* **the** *factor that hurts disabled applicants the most.)* In this case, you should try to volunteer for some internship or other on-the-job training program *(see Appendix B in* What Color Is Your Parachute?*)*. Volunteering at some place that truly interests you is also an attractive option if you are dying to work, but with your present benefit package you cannot really *afford* to take a job, lest you lose those benefits and medical coverage. By volunteering your services, you get a chance to keep your benefits, and still use your God-given talents or abilities, toward making this world a better place.

The Art of Self-Sabotage

You may have to do *many* interviews, in order to find a job. We're talking about twenty or thirty different places. Giving up after just six interviews and six turndowns is tossing in the towel *much too soon.*

When things aren't going well, you will of course want to blame it on something. *Who don't?* The first tempting target, when you have a disability, is to think that *that* is the reason you are getting turned down. And that may well be so, in this tribal world we live in--as we saw earlier. Three-quarters of all managers feel that people with disabilities *do* encounter discrimination from employers, according to the Lou Harris survey. On the other hand, most employers (the survey found) *are* willing to employ more people with disabilities *if they are qualified.*

Convincing the employer that you are qualified is *your* job, during the interview. **If you are somehow failing to do this, then it is clear that other things besides your disability are causing you to get turned down.** Facing up to this possibility shows a lot of guts. You are saying, in effect, *"I* **am responsible."** In our society, it is infinitely more popular to blame any failure *(including the failure of our job-hunt)* on **someone else.** The possibilities are endless, just so it's someone *out there* rather than yourself. It could be employers, or society, or the government, or the employment service, or the welfare system, or your counselor, or your unsympathetic family.

Of course, there's one small problem with this temptation to always blame our failures on something or someone *out there.* If *something out there* made your job-hunt fail, then you have no power to change that, whatsoever. On the other hand, if it is something *you* are doing, that is making your job-hunt not work, then there is hope--because, changing that *is* within your power and is within your grasp.

Well, okay, so **how** might you be botching up the interviews with employers? And **why** might you be botching them up? Well, *simple inexperience* in this business of interviewing for a job is one very obvious reason. Also, you may have no desire at all to go back to work (if you became disabled, for example, at a job you hated)--but you need to go through *the appearances* of job-hunting, in order to mollify your friends and family--who may be working very hard to support you, with the expectation that *this is all temporary*.

Those are the kinds of reasons we may be conscious of. And then there is that vast realm of things we may be unconscious of. We are no different from employers, in that we have our own fears. **Those fears may unconsciously cause us to self-sabotage our own job-hunt.** How? Well, there are several deliciously inventive ways of doing this. The easiest is to just play *into* the employer's fears, instead of reassuring him or her:

Fearful Employer: "If I offer you this job, how are you going to deal with this difficulty that your disability poses?"

Self-sabotaging Job-Hunter: "I'm very glad you asked me that, because personally I think it's going to be a big problem for me."

Another form of self-sabotage is to define what we are looking for in totally unrealistic terms:

Fearful Employer: "If I offer you this receptionist's job, you'll have to be able to type, and work on machines."

Self-sabotaging Job-Hunter: "Oh no, the only thing I want to do is answer the phone, take messages, and greet people."

Or, again:

Fearful Employer: "This is a Mom-and-Pop operation, and we need a bicycle repairman like yourself; but you'd have to be able to run the whole business occasionally, when I need to get away."

Self-sabotaging Job-Hunter: "Oh no, the only thing I want to do is the actual repair work on the bikes. I hate dealing with people."

Sometimes we sabotage ourselves by aiming *too high,* usually because of our identification with someone we admired. He was a policeman. So naturally, we want to be a policeperson. Twenty-twenty vision is *mandated.* We persist even though we have a serious visual impairment which will inevitably get us disqualified. Self-sabotage, again.

Well, you get the picture. If you *are* sabotaging your own job-hunt, you will have to do your best to figure out just exactly what it is that is keeping you from getting hired --*besides your disability.* Unhappily, employers will hardly ever help you out, here. You will *never* hear them say, "Something's wrong with you besides your disability," and then spell it out (e.g., "You're too cocky and arrogant during the interview"). You will always be left completely in the dark as to why you aren't getting hired. *Of course, that's true of job-hunters without disabilities too. Employers rarely give* anyone *any feedback.*

One way around this deadly silence, of course, is to *ask* for helpful feedback. This sometimes works, *so long as* you make the inquiry *real general.* For example, after you've gotten turned down at a place, you might say, "You know, I've been on thirteen interviews now, where I've gotten turned down. Is there something about me, besides my disability, that in your view is causing me not to get hired? If so, I'd really appreciate your giving me some pointers."

Most of the time you *still* won't get a frank answer. You'll just get blithering generalities or else a killing silence. This is because of employers' fear of lawsuits and such--and also because **the world in general is perishing for a lack of those who love us enough to tell us the truth.** It's not just how they deal with you; it's how they deal with every-body.

But occasionally you will run into a loving soul, an employer, who is willing to risk giving you the truth. No matter how painful it is to hear it, thank her or him, from the bottom of your heart. Their advice, seriously heeded, can bring about just the changes in your interviewing strategy that you most need. Bless them, bless them.

In the absence of any help from employers, you're on your own to figure out what you may be doing wrong. So, let's look at some of the possibilities. They all stem from one kind of fear or another, as I said. So, the real question is, **what kinds of fears make us self-sabotage our own job-hunt?**

For starters, some of us have fallen into the bad habit at home of *using* our disability to get what we want: time, attention, and love, based on the age-old principle of "the louder you sniffle, the more you get." We often get a great deal of sympathy for our helplessness, and we fear that

going to work will mean the end of this whole way of life
--which we aren't sure we *want* to give up. We are afraid
that maybe at work, people will treat us just like any other
person. *Well, what can I tell you? We have to learn to overcome
that fear.*

Another fear: sometimes we have learned, through the
long process of qualifying for disability benefits, that any
information we volunteer may be used against us. Hence,
in the job-interview, we are afraid to volunteer very much
about ourselves. Thus we come across as trying to hide
something. *Well, what can I tell you? We have to learn to overcome that fear.*

Again, sometimes we have an irrational fear of the nondisabled and don't particularly want to be around them,
as we would have to be if we went to work. *We have to learn
to overcome that fear.*

Next: if we've never held a job before, we often know
very little about the nature of the world of work, how it
performs, and what it's like; and we often have a minimum
number of nondisabled friends who could tell us. Since
we don't know appropriate social or work behaviors, we
are afraid to go into such a strange and uncharted world.
We *have to learn to overcome that fear.*

Sometimes we are afraid that if we get a job, we won't
be able to 'cut it.' *We have to learn to overcome that fear.*

And then sometimes we are afraid to face our limitations, as putting ourselves to the test at a job would force
us to do. *We have to learn to overcome that fear.*

I know, I know. All of that is easy to say. But how exactly
do we overcome our fears? Well, **practicing** helps. You do
this by taking one situation a day where your normal behavior is avoidance, based on fear, and you take a risk that

day, by acting differently than you normally would. One risk a day. With daily practice, you will get stronger and stronger. It's just like exercising your muscles.

Also, don't overlook the possibility of seeking help from your spiritual life and prayer (see the Epilogue in *Parachute* on "Finding Your Mission in Life"). That has helped some job-hunters *immeasurably,* in overcoming their fears. They learn that every experience becomes an adventure for Two: God's Spirit, and You. Together, You can overcome all fear.

Bibliography

Bolles, Richard N., *What Color Is Your Parachute? A Practical Manual for Job-Hunters & Career-Changers* (revised annually, with the new edition appearing each November). Ten Speed Press, Box 7123, Berkeley, CA 94707. Available in almost all bookstores. This is the basic manual for *all* job-hunters, whether or not they have a disability. It should be required reading for all readers of this booklet.

Azrin, Nathan H., and Besalel, Victoria A., *Job Club Counselor's Manual: A Behavioral Approach to Vocational Counseling.* Pro-Ed, 8700 Shoal Creek Blvd., Austin, TX 78758, 512-451-3246. 1980. This is not a directory, but a detailed description of a particular method of job-hunting, called "the job club." Nathan invented the job club in 1970, in order to find a more structured way in which to help persons with disabilities, as they went about their job-hunt. This manual explains in great detail how to set up such a club. Furthermore, chapter 14 in Azrin's book has a section on "Evaluation of the Job Club with Job-Handicapped Persons," which reports the success of this method with those who are disabled: 95% of those people with disabilities who were in the Job Club found jobs within 6 months, compared to 28% in a non-job-club control group. The job club's participants got salaries which were 22% higher than those in the control group who found jobs. Nathan has written another manual for disabled job-hunters who cannot find a job club near them, spelling out how to follow the job club techniques all by yourself. That book is: Azrin, Nathan H., and Besalel, Victoria A., *Finding A Job.* Ten Speed Press, P.O. Box 7123, Berkeley, CA 94707. 1982.

If you want information about what other resources exist to help you in your job-hunt, there is the **Clearinghouse on Disability Information,** U.S Department of Education, Room 3132, Switzer Bldg., Washington, DC 20202-2524, 202-732-1241. It publishes an INFOPAC on *Employment of Individuals with Disabilities,* which you may ask for, that lists all kinds of groups, agencies, and programs throughout the country that exist to assist people with disabilities in finding employment or training for employment. They also publish a list of *Selected Federal Publications Relating to Disability.* January 1989.

They also distribute *Summary of Existing Legislation Affecting Persons with Disabilities,* Publication No. E-88-22014, August 1988, that summarizes in some detail all the federal laws that protect you, serve you, or offer you help. The Clearinghouse has a simpler version of the above publication, called the *Pocket Guide to Federal Help for Individuals with Disabilities,* which you can buy from the Superintendent of Documents, U.S. Government Printing Office, Washington, DC 20402.

If the above information doesn't tell you what you want to know, the Clearinghouse also has a *Directory of National Information Sources on Handicapping Conditions and Related Services,* published May 1986, by the National Institute of Disability and Rehabilitation Research, 330 C St. SW, Room 330C, Washington, DC 20202. This directory has an addendum of address changes, etc. that have occurred up through 6/27/89. The directory and addendum are available from the Clearinghouse on Disability Information, address above. However, since this is an expensive book, see if your local library, or rehabilitation office has a copy--should you wish to browse it.

You will also want to know about Project LINK, if you live (or want to live) in or near Dallas, Texas, or Washington, DC. It is a centralized placement service for job-ready persons with disabilities, providing job development and placement to about 400 disabled individuals per year. These placements have a retention rate of about 90%. If you are interested in exploring this service, you may contact them, at either: Project LINK, Mainstream, Inc., 1030 15th St., NW, Suite 1010, Washington, DC 20005, or Project LINK, Mainstream, Inc., 717 North Harwood, Suite 890, Dallas, TX 75201.

For those desiring some information about the 300 or so independent living centers or programs in this country, there is the *Directory of Independent Living Programs,* published by Research and Training Center on Independent Living, 3400 Bissonnet, Suite 101, Houston, TX 77005. Contact Laurel Richards, 713-666-6244.

Another group approach to helping people with disabilities in their job-search is: Ryan, Colleen, *Job Search Workshop for Disabled, Dislocated and Discouraged Workers.* Adult Life Resource Center, Division of Continuing Education, The University of Kansas. 1985.

Rabby, Rami, and Croft, Diane, *Take Charge: A Strategic Guide for Blind Job Seekers.* National Braille Press Inc., 88 St. Stephen St., Boston, MA 02115. 1989. Orders must be prepaid (NBP does not invoice). Print edition: $23.95; Braille edition: $19.95. Cassette edition: $19.95. IBM disk edition (5¼" or 3½" disks): $19.95.

The ICD Survey II: Employing Disabled Americans, conducted by Louis Harris and Associates, Inc., for the International Center for the Disabled, 340 E. 24th St., New York, NY 10010. 1987.

For people with disabilities who have never been in the job-market before, and have only a limited education, there is a very useful *Guide to Basic Skills Jobs,* Vol. 1. RPM Press, Inc., Verndale, MN 56481. 1986. A catalog of viable jobs for individuals with only basic work skills. This volume identifies 5,000 major occupations within the U.S. economy which require no more than an eighth grade level of education, and no more than one year of specific vocational preparation. Immensely useful book.

McBurney Resource Center, 905 University Ave., Madison, WI 53706. Access to Independence, Inc., 1954 E. Washington Ave., Madison, WI 53704. Lists resources that help with the psychological aspects of job-hunting.

Kimeldorf, Martin, and Edwards, Jean, *Numbers That Spell Success: Transitions to Work and Leisure Roles for Mildly Handicapped Youth.* Ednick Communications, Box 3612, Portland, OR 97208. 1988.

Bowe, Frank, *Handicapping America: Barriers to Disabled People.* HarperCollins, 10 E. 53rd St., New York, NY 10022. 1978.

Klein, Karen, with Hope, Carla Derrick, *Bouncing Back From Injury: How to Take Charge of Your Recuperation.* Prima Publishing & Communications, P. O. Box 1260BB, Rocklin, CA 95677. 1988.

Freedman, Jacqueline, and Gersten, Susan, *Traveling .... Like Everybody Else: A Practical Guide for Disabled Travelers.* Adama Books, 306 W. 38 St., New York, NY 10018. 1987.

Callahan, John, *Don't Worry, He Won't Get Far on Foot: The Autobiography of a Dangerous Man.* William Morrow & Co., Inc., 1989. John became a quadriplegic at the age of 21, due to an automobile accident. However, he has a wicked sense of humor, and so has become a famous cartoonist whose cartoons regard no subject as off-limits: disabilities, sex, religion, government programs, you name it. His cartoons, and this book, are not for those whose sensibilities are easily offended. This book is John's autobiography, and it is graphic, funny and touching. Arnold Beisser (below) wrote a most relevant passage in *his* book, apropos of such 'disabled humor' as John's: "The able-bodied person is likely to be appalled by 'disabled humor' and find nothing funny at all about it. But…tragedy and comedy are but two aspects of what is real, and whether we see the tragic or the humorous is a matter of perspective." John's perspective is clearly that he prefers to see the *humorous* amid the tragedy.

"Don't worry, he won't get far on foot."

Beisser, Arnold R., *Flying Without Wings: Personal Reflections on Being Disabled*. Doubleday, 666 Fifth Ave., New York, NY 10103. 1989. This is *such* an important book, dealing as it does with one's *attitude* toward disability. As one wise man said about his disability in *The Disability Rag* (below): *"Every disabled person has the choice of either 'crying the blues' about their disability every day of their life, or realistically acknowledging what they have to do in order to have a successful, productive life."* Beisser has ultimately opted for the latter, though it was not an easy battle, as this book reveals. His wisdom and compassion are classified under such chapter headings as: *Time; Space; Relationships; The Choice;* and *Humor and Enlightenment*. This should be mandatory reading for *everyone*, but most especially for persons with disabilities who are having a hard time wrestling with their attitude toward their disability.

Journals or Periodicals:

Careers and the Handicapped, 44 Broadway, Greenlawn, NY 11740, James Schneider, ed., 516-261-8899. Published twice yearly.

The Disability Rag, Box 145, Louisville, KY 40201. An avant-garde journal dealing with all the different feelings --amid a wide range of vocabulary--that are going on within people who happen to have disabilities. Nothing is off limits. Frank and often graphic, especially in its language. Not for everyone, but has some very informative articles and debates in it.

For persons who are "print handicapped" or for other reasons can't read books or journals:

The National Library Service for the Blind and Physically Handicapped, Library of Congress, 1291 Taylor St. NW, Washington, DC 20542 has put many books on career planning and job-hunting (such as *Parachute*) on tape, which they will send, with special playback equipment, to your home and back, free, if you are able to prove a "print handicap."

Recording for the Blind, Inc., 20 Roszel Rd., Princeton, NJ 08540, likewise has translated job-hunting books for the print handicapped and visually impaired.

Also every state has library services of recorded books, usually lodged in the state library or the state agency for the blind. Any counselor, social worker, or blind person in your state should know where this is.

If there's something you're looking for, and you just can't find it locally, try the Library of Congress in Washington, DC.

IF YOU ARE NEWLY DISABLED

If you are a newly disabled or injured worker, and you have no idea what benefits there are for you in general, nor what aids exist to help you with your job-hunt, here are some suggestions as to **how you find out** what's available to you:

Talk to other people with disabilities: if you have one who is a friend, or even if you meet one on the street, go up to them and say: "I'm newly disabled; do you know of anyone who could teach me the ropes?"

Visit or call the Disabled Students program of your local community college, college, or university. They will tell you what helps there are for you.

Visit or call one of the 300 Independent Living Centers in the U.S., if there is one near you. They will know.

Visit or call the United Way. They usually maintain an information and referral directory, which includes services for the Disabled.

Visit or call your local public library, particularly its librarian or reference librarian. Say to them, "I just became disabled; could you help me find out who I can go to, that could help me with counseling and the like?" If you're on your own there in the library, look up "handicapped" or "disabled" in the card catalog and see what information or referral directories you can turn up for your local town or city.

Also, local churches or synagogues often will know about resources to help you, since frequently they have people with disabilities in their congregations.

Resources to Help You

The preceding was introductory only. A more complete listing of the resources available to help you, would include the following:

Local Resources to help you if you have a disability:

> *The local offices of the State Rehabilitation Bureau*
> *Independent Living Centers*
> *Catholic Charities*
> *Jewish Vocational Services*
> *Lutheran Family Services*
> *Organizations funded by the United Way (ask)*
> *Your local Legal Services office, for questions regarding Social Security, your eligibility, and employer responsibilities.*

Private rehab firms and counselors and nurses. These can be *immensely* helpful, but as with career counselors in general *(see Appendix C in* Parachute*)*, you will have to choose *very* carefully. The marks of a poor (or burnt-out) rehab counselor are: they have lost the ability to listen; they tend therefore to stereotype you rather than focussing on your uniqueness (you can just hear them thinking, "I've heard this one before"); they only pay lip service to the idea that you can be independent, because in their heart of hearts they really believe the disabled need to be taken care of; they know the anatomy of disabilities, but not the anatomy of abilities. Their basic need is to take care of people, and they set this personal need of theirs ahead of your best interests.

On the other hand, the marks of a **good** rehab counselor are: they have excellent rapport with their clients; they have high expectations of their clients; they feel it is in the client's best interest that the client should make the decisions concerning his or her life; their clients accomplish a great deal. They familiarize themselves with your file, if you have seen other counselors previously, but they do not accept other people's judgments about you, unless or until they see that behavior for themselves. If they have a personality conflict with a client, they refer them immediately to someone more helpful in that situation. Furthermore, they research thoroughly what the disability is, rather than accepting cliches about it. Their basic need is **to act as a facilitator** for you, and their major contribution to your job-hunt is that they are skilled at helping you identify your abilities and then identifying a job which asks for just those abilities, so that when it comes time for you to fill out an application form at some company or organization, and you come to the question, "Do you have any disability that would keep you from performing *this* job?" you can truthfully answer "No."

If you have a counselor already, but after reading this paragraph feel you've unwittingly fallen into the wrong hands, see if you can 'redeem them' (for example, if they keep limiting what you can do with such statements as "Don't do that, you'll lose this benefit or that," ask them for *written facts,* that you can take home and study). If you can't redeem them, make your exit firmly and finally; and seek another.

State Resources to help you if you have a disability:

Your State offices of human services (they go under various titles, in the individual states). They can usually assist you in determining which state agencies might be helpful to you.

The State Department of Rehabilitation or Rehabilitation Bureau in your State (probably headquartered in the city that is the State Capital). They can be important if you are trying to get hired by a small company, since *sometimes* the State Department or Bureau is in a position to help buy equipment needed to help you function in that particular job.

The Employment Development Department or Job Service in your state. Some offices have job centers for persons with disabilities, and/or veteran's assistance centers.

Social Security offices. All local offices *should* have a work incentives liaison, including PASS (Plan to Achieve Self Support) and other incentives. Ask if they apply to you.

The state or national committee for your disability, e.g.,

United Cerebral Palsy
Strokes
Epilepsy
Association for Retarded Citizens

Regional centers for the Developmentally Disabled (usually defined as those who were disabled before the age of 18 years or so, though the definition varies from place to place).

Protection and Advocacy groups in major cities which function as ombudsman or legal advocacy persons, on behalf of former mental patients and others.

Federal or National Resources to help you
if you have a disability:

Laws. The Americans With Disabilities Act of 1990 (ADA) requires that all employers with **15** or more employees, must comply with the following laws by July 26,

1994: They must provide 'reasonable accommodation,' including job restructuring and modification of equipment, to individuals with disabilities, unless such accommodations would impose an 'undue hardship' on the business operations. They must not discriminate in hiring or promotion against a person otherwise qualified for the job, just because that person has a disability. They are allowed to ask about one's ability to perform the job, but cannot inquire if one has a disability--or use tests that tend to screen out people with disabilities. *Incidentally, employers with 25 or more employees must comply with the above laws by July 26, 1992.*

Your congressperson. They usually have a social worker on their staff, who is often able to help you if you're running into some kind of a dead-end locally. What you can tell them, for example, is: "I'm a person with *this* disability, and I'm trying to find *this* kind of job, so I've located prospective employers, but this is the problem I'm running into ...." Sometimes there's nothing they can do, but other times they can be small miracle workers.

The President's Committee on Employment of Persons with Disabilities, 1111 20th St. NW, Washington, DC 20202.

National Council on Disability, 800 Independence Ave. SW, Suite 814, Washington, DC 20591.

The Office of Special Education and Rehabilitative Services, U.S. Dept. of Education, Room 3225, Switzer Bldg., 330 C St. SW, Washington, DC 20202.

The U.S. Department of Education, Office of Special Education & Rehabilitative Services

The Job Training Partnership Act (JTPA)

For *further* information on resources that may be able to help you, see the resources available from the Clearing-house on Disability Information, referred to earlier.

A P. S. to Employers: *Do use employees with disabilities to the fullest of their abilities; don't put them in a repetitious, safe, dead-end job, just so that you won't have to spend any time on them. If you hire someone with a disability, be prepared especially to give them some time and attention during the training period. Since many employers are prone to take shortcuts in this area with* **all** *their employees, hiring someone with a disability can have a salutary effect on your whole organization, as you have impressed upon you anew the importance of training for all.*

If any of your employees with disabilities aren't working out, tell them so, early on. If problems arise with their performance, don't wait too long to intervene. There are problems that can be solved, if they are tackled early enough, and tackled jointly.

If the person you hire screws up on the job, don't blame it on their disability. Blame it, as you would with any other employee, on human nature. If you have to let them go, again don't blame it on the disability or start gossip with other employers you know, along the lines of, "Well I hired a disabled person, but it just didn't work." One poor employee who has a disability doesn't say anything about other employees with disabilities. It's better to stop such gossip before it starts.

If a nondisabled person at your company becomes disabled, do go and visit them. A visit from you is important. Say, "We miss you, and we want you back." If you are in a position to offer some economic help toward getting them back on their feet, do it. Your organization will realize cost savings by getting this trained and devoted employee back on the job, even in modified or alternative work.

Acknowledgments

The following people helped me in one way or another with this booklet, and their assistance and generosity is *gratefully* acknowledged--though, needless to say, they are not responsible for any of the opinions contained herein, nor for any errors that may be found:

Ed Roberts, President and Co-founder of the World Institute on Disability (WID), Berkeley, California; **Judy Heumann,** Vice-president and Co-founder of WID; **Maud Steyaert,** Administrative Asst., WID; **Chuck Young,** Administrator, Oregon Commission for the Blind, Portland, Oregon; **Pam Maxon,** Employment Specialist, Oregon Commission for the Blind; **Linda Blake,** Executive Director, Independent Living Resource, Pleasant Hill, California; **Betty Zarn,** Resource Specialist, ILR, Pleasant Hill; **John Wingate,** Executive Director, International Center for the Disabled, New York, N.Y.; **Marshall Karp,** Director, New Career, Dover, Ohio; **Sidney Fine,** 'father' of the Dictionary of Occupational Titles, Milwaukee, Wisconsin; **Nathan Azrin,** 'father' of Job Clubs, Nova University, Fort Lauderdale, Florida; **Barbara Mitchell,** Job Club Coordinator, Dept. of Rehabilitation, San Rafael (California) Office; **Ms. Terry Stimpson,** Rehabilitation Counselor, Stimpson Associates, Mountain View, California; **Judy Gelwicks,** Judith Gelwicks & Co., Gilroy, California; **James Jackson,** Veterans Representative, EDD Pleasant Hill (California) Office; **Zack Blake,** Office Director, Deaf Counseling, Advocacy, and Referral Agency (DCARA), EDD Pleasant Hill (California) Office; and **Martha Server,** Job Placement Specialist, Mirfak Associates, Inc., Oakland, California.

Other Resources

Additional materials by Richard N. Bolles to help you with your job-hunt:

THE 1992 WHAT COLOR IS YOUR PARACHUTE?
A Practical Manual for Job-Hunters & Career-Changers

"Everyone agrees that the giant title in the field is Richard N. Bolles's What Color Is Your Parachute?, *which first appeared in 1972 and has been updated annually ever since." —The New York Times*

6×9 inches, 448 pages. $12.95 paper, $17.95 cloth

THE ANATOMY OF A JOB

This 24×36-inch color picture of the "Flower" (see 1992 *Parachute*, p. 225) gives you room to write your responses to the exercises in Appendix A there. Being able to put all the information on one page and in order of priority helps you stay on track during the informational interviewing phase of your job-hunt. $4.95

HOW TO CREATE A PICTURE OF YOUR IDEAL JOB OR NEXT CAREER

This 8½ by 11-inch version of Appendix A in *Parachute* is available as a separate booklet. The larger format makes working the exercises in Appendix A much easier. $5.95

HOW TO FIND YOUR MISSION IN LIFE

This is a gift book version of the current Epilogue in *Parachute*. Judging by the mail Dick Bolles receives, this is a favorite of readers who want their work to fulfill a purpose and bring more than simply money to their lives. $5.95

To: Ten Speed Press
P.O. Box 7123
Berkeley, CA 94707

I would like to order:

_____ copies of **THE 1992 WHAT COLOR IS YOUR PARACHUTE?** @ ☐ $12.95, paper
☐ $17.95, cloth   _____

_____ copies of the poster **THE ANATOMY OF A JOB** @ $4.95 each   _____

_____ copies of **HOW TO CREATE A PICTURE OF YOUR IDEAL JOB OR NEXT CAREER** @ $5.95 each   _____

_____ copies of **JOB-HUNTING TIPS FOR THE SO-CALLED "HANDICAPPED" OR PEOPLE WHO HAVE DISABILITIES** @ $4.95 each   _____

_____ copies of **HOW TO FIND YOUR MISSION IN LIFE** @ $5.95 each   _____

Subtotal $_____

Postage is $1.50 for the first item ordered
and $1.00 for *each* additional item.

Postage $_____

Total $_____

Check or money order only, please, made out to Ten Speed Press.

Send to:

(please print)

Name_____

Organization_____

Mailing Address_____

City, State, Zip_____